Shopping for The Perfect Grant

Diane Winbush

ISBN-13:

978-1533122360

ISBN-10:

1533122369

Copyright © 2016 by Diane Winbush

Resources by: Grant.gov

®All Rights Reserved

Copyrighting is prohibited of the contents of this book

Table of Contents

Chapter One	Defining A Grant
Chapter Two	Why Apply
Chapter Three	When should I Apply
Chapter Four	Getting Prepared
Chapter Five	Applying for College Grant
Chapter Six	Applying for a Personal Grant
Chapter Seven	Applying for a small Bus. Grant
Chapter Eight	Am I Eligible
Chapter Nine	Where to search for a Grant
Chapter Ten	Grant Fraud

Chapter One

Defining A Grant

Apply for a Grant

Grants can be difficult to receive approval for at times. This book will provide the contents and information which is needed to apply and to learn what a grant is.

A grant is Grants are non-repayable funds or products disbursed by one party (grant makers), often a government department, corporation, foundation or trust, to a recipient, often (but not always) a nonprofit entity, educational institution, business or an individual. In order to receive a grant, some form of "Grant Writing" often referred to as either a proposal or an application is required.

Most grants are made to fund a specific project and require some level of compliance and reporting. The grant writing process involves an applicant submitting a proposal (or submission) to a potential funder, either on the applicant's own initiative or in response to a Request for Proposal from the funder.

Other grants can be given to individuals, such as victims of natural disasters or individuals who seek to open a small business. Sometimes grant makers require grant seekers to have some form of tax-exempt status, be a registered nonprofit organization or a local government.

For example, tiered funding for a freeway are very large grants negotiated at government policy level. However smaller grants may be provided by a government agency (e.g. municipal government).

Project-related funding involving business, communities, and individuals is often arranged by application either in writing or online.

Most entrepreneurs and business owners apply for grants without learning their own purpose for applying or that it's free money. Grants are much more than that.

Chapter Two

Why Apply for A Grant?

Do you have a purpose in mind as to why you are applying for a grant? There are all sorts of reasons why entrepreneurs are applying.

This is very important because grantees will know your true purpose for applying. Those whom are requesting a grant should have a general mission and vision for apply.

It can sound and look great, but the goals and plan must align with your purpose for applying.

In a sentence: grants enable you to do work you might never do otherwise. Community projects take time. Unless you are wealthy, you cannot pay staff salaries -- or your own salary -- from your own pocket. And few of us are able to buy expensive equipment, or cover a year's worth of office expenses, without outside help. So in many situations, grants are desirable; in some, they are essential.

Many situations, but not all:

- There are times when you can do excellent community work with very little money, or no money at all.

Organizing a meeting, holding a social event, getting local policies changed -- these and similar community actions are either cost-free, or come with very modest price tags.

- There are also times when money can become an actual drawback. Someone has to figure out how to spend it, make the payments, keep the records, and be accountable for it. Also, when you have money, your own members may compete for it; the all-volunteer, let's-everyone-pitch-in spirit of the project may be impeded.

And although grants are an excellent way to generate money, they are not the only one. They might belong in your financial planning, but your financial plan should also include other sources of income. A grant might be your guest of honor; but don't you want others to come to your party?

Ask yourself these questions, and check your answers:

- What are my true long-term program goals here?
- Can I do the same work as well, or almost as well, without grant money?
- What will I actually use the dollars for?

- Am I planning to apply simply because grant funds are potentially available?
- Is a grant the only way (or the best way) to do what I want to do?
- Are there other (and perhaps better) ways of getting the money I need?
- Am I clear on my realistic chances of success?
- Am I prepared to put in the work to produce a top-quality grant proposal?

Chapter Three

When Should You Apply for A Grant?

Business owners can apply at the incorrect time for a grant. As I lectured a previous workshop; I illustrated this example to the attendants.

Susie decides to open a business in the flower shop industry. Flowers has been a trade of Susie for years. She opens her flower business with six clients. She provides high quality work for her customers.

Susie's clients tell their friends of the flower business and Susie gains two more clients for business.

Susie drives a 2016 Bonneville. She has utilized her mid-sized car since she opened her business to deliver her products and services.

Due to Susie gaining two more clients; should she purchase a new vehicle since her business is growing?

I advised our attendants that the flowers can be transported in the vehicle until a larger vehicle is needed. The same concept applies for when to apply for a grant.

If there is no need to apply; let the funds remain until the opportunity presents to apply for one.

Remember; the time and efforts of preparing a grant will be a great reflect on you and your business. Make sure that you need the grant.

When you want to start a new project, or expand an existing project, and financial costs are involved

- When these costs cannot be covered in your current budget
- When you know of a granting agency that makes awards to pay for the types of costs you envision
- When you know that you meet the eligibility standards for such awards
- When you are able to commit the needed time and energy to the grant-writing process

Chapter Four

Getting Prepared

Apply for a Grant

You can identify potential grant funding opportunities by searching the federal government's grant website located at: http://www.grants.gov/web/grants/search-grants.html.

- The website allows you to search by keyword, funding opportunity number or CFDA (Catalog for Federal Domestic Assistance) Number, which is the five-digit number assigned to the grant by the federal government.

- If you are searching for new grant opportunities, perform a keyword search that best reflects your business products, research areas or business needs.

- Quickly review the search results by clicking on the Funding Opportunity Number, which is a hyperlink that will redirect you to additional information about the grant. There will be four hyperlink tabs (Synopsis, Version History, Related Documents and Package), read through the description of the grant to determine whether it meets your needs.

•Once you have preliminarily identified a list of potential grants, closely read the grant's eligibility section and the full announcement to determine whether you meet the requirements, scope of work or research parameters of the grant. You can review the full announcement and other supporting documents by selection the Related Documents Tab and then clicking on the relevant documents.

Once you have determined that you meet the eligibility and scope of work requirements, download the grant application. •You can download the grant application by selecting the Application tab and then by selection the "select package" hyperlink listed under "Actions." You will be prompted to provide your email address to receive grant updates and then given the option to download the materials.

•You can also download grant application packages by entering the grant's Funding Opportunity Number or CFDA Number here: https://apply07.grants.gov/apply/forms_apps_idx.html.

- The benefit of downloading a grant application package is that it allows you to complete and review your materials offline before submitting the finished application.

Register with Grants.gov. In order to submit a grant application, you must register with grants.gov as either an individual or business applicant. You can register online at:http://www.grants.gov/web/grants/register.html. Generally, you will need to provide the following information: •As an individual registrant, you must know funding number of the grant for which you are applying. You can enter the funding number at this website:

https://apply07.grants.gov/apply/IndCPRegister and then click the "register" button. You will be redirected to a registration form which you will fill out and that will prompt you to create a username and password.

- Organizations registering with the grant website must first obtain a DUNS number, which is a nine-digit business identifying number.

You can register online at: https://fedgov.dnb.com/webform/pages/CCRSearch.jspr or call 1-866-705-5711.

You will need the following information to get your DUNS number: your legal name; the name and address of your business headquarters; any other organization names used by your business; the mailing address if different from the physical or business address; and a business telephone number, contact name and title. You may also need to provide the number of employees at your organization.

- Organizations must also register with the System Award Management (SAM). You can register at https://www.sam.gov by providing the name of your organization's authorizing official of your organization and an Employer Identification Number (EIN).

- Organizations can complete their Authorized Organization Representative (AOR) profile and create a username and password by using their DUNS number to register here: https://apply07.grants.gov/apply/OrcRegister

- You must then use your username and password to log into grants.gov in order to request access and approval.

Once you complete these steps and you are approved, your organization will be registered with Grants.gov and able to submit grant applications.

Review instructions.

Each grant will provide you with instructions in addition to the grant application materials. You must closely review the instructions when preparing your grant proposal.

- Instructions on how to open and use the forms in the package are on the application package cover sheet. #*Agency specific instructions can be downloaded with your application and will include information required for your submission.

Write your grant materials. Most grants require that you submit a grant proposal that clearly shows how you meet all of the grant's requirements, a budget and what you intend to accomplish with the grant money.

You can review sample documents provided above. Generally, your proposal should include:

- Information that meets all of the requirements of the grant.

- A typo-free and grammatically correct document that persuasively sets forth your project aims.

- Check for formatting requirements, such as font and page limits, and be sure to follow those requirements exactly.

- Any documents that were required or that support your grant application such as tax documents or business documents.

Submit the completed Grant Application Package. Once you have finalized your materials, you are ready to submit your grant. • Open the finalized grant application and click the "save" button located on the grant application cover page.

- Next, click "save" button on the cover page.

- You will have the opportunity to click a "Check Package for Errors" button. You should use this option as the system will let you know if you have included all of the required information. Correct any errors that the system finds.

- **Click the "Save & Submit" button and save the application. You will only have this option once all errors have been rectified. You must save the application in order to begin the submission process.**

- **Once you select "Save & Submit," you will be prompted to enter your username and password. You will be provided instructions on how to finalize your submission.**

- **Once your submission is complete, the system will provide you with confirmation information and a tracking number for your submission. Be sure to save this information.**

Track your application. You can track the status of your application by entering the tracking number at the following website: http://www.grants.gov/web/grants/applicants/track-my-application.html.

The system will tell you if your application was received but will not tell you whether you were awarded the grant. This information will come directly from the agency awarding the grant money.

Chapter Five

Applying for A College Grant?

Apply for a Grant

Choose a college that is a right fit and accepts Pell grants. Choosing the right college is an important decision. The amount of financial aid you receive may help you narrow down your choices. Pell grants are financial awards given based on economic need to low-income undergraduates and some students seeking degrees beyond college.

If you think that you may qualify for a Pell grant, consider the following:

•Pell grants do not need to be repaid like student loans. Therefore, if you qualify for a Pell grant you can significantly reduce the amount of your college tuition with no further financial repayment obligation.

•When choosing a college, you should check with the school's financial aid office to make sure that they participate in the Pell grant program.

•When researching schools, be sure to identify the Federal School Code for each school so that you can include it on your financial aid application. By identifying this information before filling your application, you ensure that your financial aid information is sent directly to those schools. You can locate Federal School Codes at https://fafsa.ed.gov/FAFSA/app/schoolSearch?locale=en_EN here.

Fill out a FAFSA or Free Application for Federal Student Aid. This form can be found at. The FAFSA contains questions that ask about you, your financial information, your school plans, etc.

File early! Many federal education grants are offered on a first-come, first-served basis, so the sooner you submit your FAFSA after January 1, the better your chances are to receive a grant.

Fill out the application. Be sure to double check all information before hitting "submit". If necessary, you can save your information at any point in the application. To save your application, click the SAVE button at the bottom of any FAFSA page. Your saved application will be automatically deleted after 45 days or after the federal application/correction deadline date has passed.

View your results online! Carefully review the Student Aid Report (SAR) that you'll receive in response to submitting your FAFSA. These results will tell you if you're eligible for a Pell Grant, and if so, for how much money. You can also make corrections to a processed FAFSA if necessary.

Follow the instructions for claiming your Pell Grant money. If you have questions, it is best to reach out to the Federal Student Aid Information Center at 1-800-4-FED-AID or speak with a representative at your school's financial aid office.

Chapter Six

Applying for A Personal Grant

Apply for a Grant

If you are looking for a grant to finance a personal research project, you might not think to look to the government. The U.S. Department of Health and Human Services administers its web site, www.grants.gov.

Although the vast majority of these grants are only available to state agencies and non-profit organizations, a few of them might be open to you as an individual applicant. More than 26 federal agencies post their grants on this web site, so it is definitely worth investigating.

Search for eligible grants. There are thousands of federal grants available to search for on-line, but most of them are designed for organizations and governmental agencies.

You should not waste time applying for these as an individual because you will be quickly deemed ineligible.

- When you go onto the grants.gov web site, be sure to first check the box labeled "Individuals" under the Eligibility section. This will filter out the results so you only see grants you are eligible to win.

Read the descriptions of each grant. Many federal grants for individuals are specific in scope. They may be designed to help an individual conduct research or help complete a project at a federal institution (like the Department of Energy).

They are also often designed to help strengthen relationships between the federal government and an international population living in the United States.

If you are looking for a grant to help pay off personal debt -- as in a credit card or student loan debt -- it is unlikely you will find this through the federal government.

Make a list of eligible grants. Because the grants are often very specific in nature, it is unlikely you will be a good fit for more than one.

But you should still keep a list of the grants you plan to apply to so you can stay organized during the application process.

You should keep this list in an accessible place, like a notebook that you use frequently or save this list on your computer. Consider backing up your documents in cloud space like Dropbox or Google Cloud, Google Drive, One Drive, Box and more.

Chapter Seven

Applying for a Government Grant for Small Business

Apply for a Grant

Learn the requirements to apply for a government small business grant. The government allots grant amounts according to the size and type of organization or business. Grants are given to individuals, nonprofit organizations, education organizations, housing organizations, and Native American organizations. Small business grants are allotted according to the size and standard of the business. Assess the categorization and size of your business and check it against government guidelines found at grants.gov.

For example, many opportunities for grants involve medical research or early childhood education. Choose a grant opportunity that most closely matches your organization's size and expertise. Stay true to your mission and don't try to create a program just for grant funding.

Find open government grant opportunities for small businesses. At grants.gov you can browse requests for grant proposals by category, by government agency, or by eligibility. Choose "Browse Eligibility," and then click on "Small Businesses." Review all grant opportunities and choose the one that best fits your organization's purpose and capabilities.

Register your organization. You must register your organization with the federal government's grant program before you can apply for grants. The application process is done online at grants.gov and can be completed in three days to three weeks. Be sure to complete all steps of the process in full, because incomplete information can make the process take much longer. In order to apply, you must have completed the following:

Obtain a DUNS (Dunn & Bradstreet) number by calling 866-705-5711 or access the Dun & Bradstreet website.

- **Register with the System Award Management (SAM). Go to https://www.sam.gov. You'll need the authorizing official of your organization and an Employer Identification Number (EIN). Obtain the EIN number from your state's Department of Finance.**

- **Complete the Authorized Organization Representative (AOR) profile and create your username and password. You'll need your organization's DUNS Number for this part.**

- **Obtain approval for the Authorized Organization Representative (AOR). Log in to grants.gov to confirm you are the AOR.**

- Log in to grants.gov and look at the Applicant Center welcome box for your current status in order to track the progress of your registration.

Review all tutorial information. At grants.gov, click on the "Learn Grants" tab and read all information on eligibility, grant terminology, how to find funding, etc. Knowing this information will greatly improve your chances of obtaining a grant.

Complete the small business grant application. At grants.gov find the grant for which you're applying, click the "Application Package" tab, then download the application package and instructions. As you are applying as a business, it's important to make sure the grants you apply for are intended for organizations, not individuals, and that you apply as a business entity and not as one person.

These types of grants are categorized separately by the government and applying for grants that are intended for sole individuals on behalf of your business will slow down the application process and could cause your grant to be rejected.

Answer all questions completely. Write your proposal and fill out all the required forms, fields, and certifications. Save frequently, as the website does not automatically save changes.

Common questions you will be asked when applying for a government small business grant will include: why you are applying for the grant, how much debt your business has, the nature of your business, how the grant money will be used, which financial managers within your company will be handling the grant money, and how the work done by your company or organization with the grant money will benefit your community.

Execute a similar program with other funding. Nothing succeeds like success, as the old saying goes.

If you can demonstrate you were successful in performing similar work in the past and can measure the positive results, you will have a better chance of receiving a government small business grant.

Ensure you have strong financials. The grant administrators will be looking for financially healthy organizations that can describe in detail how the grant money will be spent. You will also need to be able to demonstrate you have the manpower to follow all the guidelines and reporting requirements to do what you propose in your grant application.

Track the status of your small business grant application. Go to grants.gov and use the name, password and identification number given to you upon completion of the registration process.

This will allow you to see the status of your grant application and to get information about how to proceed with the process once your grant application has either been denied or approved for funding.

Contact the Small Business Administration. If your application is denied, your local Small Business Administration office will have information on how to obtain a low-interest loan or other financial assistance programs.

Your state or county may also offer grants for employee training, new construction, or tax abatements, especially if you can show you will be creating new jobs. Contact your state's Department of Finance for more information.

Investigate other government funding opportunities. As one example, the Small Business Innovation Research Program (SBIR) is a grant program that helps qualified small businesses involved in research and development.

The program was designed to encourage high tech innovation, and is limited to American-owned and independently operated for-profit businesses that have a principal researcher and less than 500 employees.

Currently there are 11 Federal departments and agencies that are required to reserve a portion of their R&D budgets for SBIR grants to small businesses.

Chapter Eight

Am I Eligible?

Apply for a Grant

Who is Eligible?

Determining whether you are eligible to apply for and receive a federal grant is very important. If you are not legally eligible for a specific funding opportunity, you would waste a lot of time and money completing the application process when you cannot actually receive the grant.

When considering eligibility, the first step is to know what type of organization you represent (or whether you are applying as an individual). If you already know whether you will apply on behalf of your organization or as an individual, then you are ready to check your eligibility.

There are many types of organizations generally eligible to apply for funding opportunities on Grants.gov.

Each type of organization listed in the categories below is a specific search criterion in Search Grants. Individual applicants are welcome too!

Government Organizations

- State governments
- County governments
- City or township governments
- Special district governments
- Native American tribal governments (federally recognized)
- Native American tribal governments (other than federally recognized)

Education Organizations

- Independent school districts
- Public and state controlled institutions of higher education
- Private institutions of higher education

Public Housing Organizations

- Public housing authorities
- Indian housing authorities

Nonprofit Organizations

- **Nonprofits having a 501(c)(3) status with the Internal Revenue Service (IRS), other than institutions of higher education**

- **Nonprofits that do not have a 501(c)(3) status with the IRS, other than institutions of higher education**

For-Profit Organizations

- **Organizations other than small businesses**

Small Businesses

Small business grants may be awarded to companies meeting the size standards established by the U.S. Small Business Administration (SBA) for most industries in the economy.

Individuals

Individual people may submit applications for a funding opportunity on their own behalf (i.e., not on behalf of a company, organization, institution, or government).

If you are registered as an individual, you are only allowed to apply to funding opportunities that are open to individuals.

Most of the funding opportunities on Grants.gov are for organizations, not individuals. If you are looking for personal financial assistance or other types of funding, check out the Grant Programs section to learn about how to find other forms of funding from the government.

Foreign Applicants

The authorizing legislation and agency policies will determine whether a foreign individual or organization may apply for the grant. Foreign applicants need to complete the same registration process as domestic applicants, but there are additional steps to this registration process.

Depending on the intended usage of the grant you are applying for, you may need to file a U.S. tax return which requires a Taxpayer Identification Number (TIN), also referred to as an employer Identification Number (EIN).

If a non-resident alien is awarded funding to perform activities outside the United States, then this likely does not constitute U.S. source income and a TIN/EIN is not necessary. Examples of such funding include scholarships, fellowship grants, targeted grants, and achievement awards.

Before applying, foreign applicants should thoroughly review the IRS website and search for their most recent guidance for Aliens and International Taxpayers.

Chapter Nine

Where to Search for A Grant?

Apply for a Grant

Finding Grant Programs

If you are just entering the realm of grants and government funding, it can feel overwhelming trying to find the right program for you or your organization. When considering grants, these programs can be broadly categorized as those awarded by the federal government and those awarded by non-federal entities. Within these two categories are a variety of funding sources and program types.

Federal Grants, Funding & Benefit Programs

To sort through the federal grant programs, the authoritative source is the Catalog of Federal Domestic Assistance (CFDA). This catalog lists all of the available funding programs to all levels of government, nonprofit organizations, for-profit businesses, and other eligible entities. Search Grants within Grants.gov allows you to search, filter, and apply for specific opportunities to receive funding from one of these programs.

Non-Federal Grant Programs

There are a large number of nonprofit organizations and for-profit businesses that also provide grants or other types of funding assistance.

Note: The information below is not exhaustive, and Grants.gov is not affiliated with, nor endorsing, any of these resources. They are provided as a convenience to prospective grant applicants.

The Foundation Center Click to View Exit Disclaimer maintains a comprehensive database on U.S. and global grant-makers and their funding opportunities.

It also operates research, education, and training programs designed to advance knowledge of philanthropy at every level.

The Funding Information Network Click to View Exit Disclaimer facilitates access to grant resources and publications to under-resourced entities and populations.

State and regional directories can also be found with some research. Try using the Community Foundation Locator Click to View Exit Disclaimer to find a grant-making foundation in your region. You may also use your preferred web search engine to find your state's grant or foundation directory. Local libraries may have access to subscription-based search engines or the Foundation Center Cooperating Collections, so visit your library to work with them for assistance.

Visit the Community Central section to learn more about the organizations, agencies, associations, and other key actors that comprise the grants community.

This is a helpful area for learning about possible partnerships and opportunities to help shape the grants world in the future.

Grants.gov Online User Guide — contains instructions for posting opportunity synopses, creating and modifying application templates, downloading submitted applications, and more.

- **Standard Language Describing the Grants.gov Application Process** — customizable copy for internal and external communications about Grants.gov

- **Grantor FAQs** — answers to grantors' most common questions.

- **Grants.gov Presentation Request Form** - If you would like to request brochures or a complimentary Grants.gov presentation on the Find and Apply process, please fill out this form and submit it to support@grants.gov.

How to Ensure a Smooth Application Submission Process.

The following practices will help to ensure that your agency's application submission process runs as smoothly as possible:

1. Encourage your applicants to register with Grants.gov.

A primary reason application submissions are rejected is that the person submitting the application has not completed the Grants.gov registration process.

It is recommended that grantors provide applicants with an overview of the process in the announcement instructions. For customizable copy about the registration process, please see "Standard Language Describing the Grants.gov Application Process."

PRO TIP: Our analysis shows that agencies with opportunity announcements that include language about the Grants.gov registration process are less likely to have applications rejected due to registration or AOR role assignment issues.

2. Accurately estimate the expected number of applications.

When indicating the Expected Number of Applications, agencies should strive to be as accurate as possible.

PRO TIP: If you are posting a new opportunity announcement, use the response to a similar funding opportunity to gauge the Expected Number of Applications.

3. Provide an Agency Contact for electronic access problems and questions.

Some agencies are incorrectly inserting "Grants.gov Help Desk" as the Agency Contact when posting an announcement. The intent of these fields is to connect the applicant to someone within your program office who can assist them when they have questions about your specific announcement. Here are how the following fields should be used:

- **Agency Contact:** This field is pre-populated by the system and contains the name of the person who is currently logged into the system and trying to publish an opportunity. This information can be overwritten as needed.

- **Email Address:** This is also pre-populated by the system and can be overwritten. Enter the email address of someone – within your agency – who can assist applicants with specific inquiries.

- **Email Description:** Enter text that will be used as a hyperlink to the email address provided. For example, if you entered "Agency Help Desk," then when the synopsis is published and someone clicks on "Agency Help Desk" an email will open with the agency contact's email address pre-populated in the "To" field.

PRO TIP: Identify someone within your program office who can serve as a contact person for prospective applicants who have questions about specific announcements.

Chapter Ten

Grant Fraud

Apply for a Grant

You Can Help Fight Fraudulent Activity

Every year, hundreds of billions of dollars are distributed in the form of federal grants to universities, local governments, organizations and individuals.

The vast majority of these funds are spent as intended, but misuse, deceit and abuse are nonetheless present. As a result, hundreds of thousand dollars go to waste.

Fraudulent behavior can take the form of embezzlement, theft, bribery or false claims and statements. Such violations of federal law are difficult to flag without the help of individuals inside the grant community.

Learn how you can help to stop fraudulent behavior and, thus, strengthen the integrity of the federal grant system and increase the overall efficiency of the government.

What is grant fraud?

Grant fraud typically occurs when award recipients attempt to deceive the government about their spending of award money. Such behavior amounts to "lying, cheating and stealing," according to the Department of Justice.

• Learn more about the responsibilities of entities that receive federal grant funds.

What is a grant scam?

The allure of so-called "free money" from the federal government has enabled scam artists to prey on people's hopes by promising access to grants — often for a fee. In reality, federal grants are rarely awarded to individuals seeking personal benefits, and applying for a grant is completely free.

• Learn how to sniff out a grant-related scam.

• Read the latest grant scam alerts.

What are the costs of grant fraud?

Besides triggering lost efficiency and waste in the government, grant fraud can also have a significant impact on entities found to have carried it out. The Department of Justice Office of the Inspector General warns that consequences can include "debarment from receiving future funding, administrative recoveries of funds, civil law suits and criminal prosecution."

Who is responsible for monitoring fraudulent behavior?

Federal Inspectors General (IG) within each government agency have been established as independent and objective units tasked with combating waste, fraud, and abuse in their respective programs.

When fraud is suspected, other government entities, such as the Federal Bureau of Investigation and the Financial Fraud Enforcement Task Force, may get involved.

- To report a suspected instance of grant fraud, contact the IG within the appropriate agency.

How can grant fraud be stopped?

Only with your help! The front line of defense against fraudulent behavior in the grant community includes accountants, auditors and other award recipient personnel.

• Access a range of resources designed to help identify and prevent grant scams and fraud.

Summary

We have shared with you the most effective tips and tools for applying for a grant. This funding can be very resourceful for your business to become successful in future and present projects.

Taking your time to research and learn more of how a grant can be useful for your project, business, organization, or company can allow you to become much closer in an approval for your grant proposal.

www.ingramcontent.com/pod-product-compliance
Lightning Source LLC
Chambersburg PA
CBHW050803180526
45159CB00004B/1537